S0-BDM-950

Elisabeth Dunker

FINE LITTLE DAY

Ideas, collections and interiors

PAVILION

Contents

My story   6
Fine Little Day   8

THE STUDIO   10
Granliden mittens   16
Mogu   18

COLLECTING   26
Beaded baskets   30
Blue crockery   36
Books   38

AT HOME   40
Kitchen   42
Bedroom   48
Living room   52
Picture wall   54

RE-USING   62
Sri Lankan doormats   64
Book clocks   66
Block-printing   68
Patchwork quilt   70
Potholder blankets   72
Decorating books   76
Wooden spoons   78
Painting textiles   82

THE CABIN   84
Småland   86
The chicken shed   90
Cobbled doilies   94
More patchwork   96

MAKING   118
Mobile   119
Crochet potholder   120
How to make a beaded jar   122
Pressing plants   124
Cutting paper   128

PEEKING IN   130
Annacate   131
Håkan and Åsa Wettre   134
Anna Backlund   138
The strawberry walk   142
Marianne Hallberg   146

PLAYING, PLAYING
AND MORE PLAYING   150
Essentials   152
Henning Trollbäck   154
Doll's house   158

WORK   162
House of Rym   164
Kauniste   170

BIG THANKS!   172

my story

I like things that are sprawling, mismatched and fragmentary; things I know nothing about. Things that are crooked, cracked, unpredictable, patinated – OK, I might have gone a bit over the top there! But I certainly love mess; unexplained, irrational, playful, naïve and unreciprocated; but also unfinished, impulsive, intuitive and preferably manic. This could be some mode of self-defence because I rarely manage to keep my sheets free from smudges and stains, I never have enough patience to sew both zigzag and straight stitch, and because structure and logic never did float my boat. Or maybe that's just the way things have been from the very beginning, I can't quite remember.

Growing up I was a shy and insecure child, despite being the eldest of four sisters. We lived in a rented flat in Sandviken, an industrial town in the province of Gästrikland, Sweden. From what I can remember, I played on my own a lot. I liked drawing paper dolls and making paper houses with slits in the beds so it looked like the dolls were lying underneath the duvets. I rarely ventured outside as I was scared of everything most of the time. Luckily things got a bit better as I got older, and when I was 14, I developed an interest in photography. Well, that is partly true, deep down it was actually about something completely different. We were a working-class family with limited resources. We didn't own any books, apart from the occasional children's book, and neither did we have a camera; the few photographs that exist of me as a child were taken by relatives or friends of the family.

When I found out that I would be allowed to borrow a camera through a photography course at school, I signed up. Apart from learning how to take photographs, we would be taught how to develop film, and talk about techniques and photography. But I wasn't at all interested in the technicalities or in working in a darkroom. I didn't care about the history

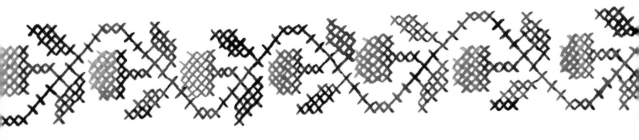

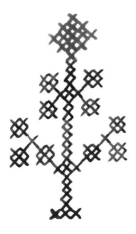

of photography and was even reluctant to look at other people's pictures. My focus was on... myself. I wanted to try and make pictures featuring me, and more importantly, myself looking attractive.

A sad and embarrassing obsession you might think, but believe me, it was a very strong driving force: I had an unfulfilled desire to try and achieve an identity that I desperately wanted, but that I just hadn't been born with. I cultivated my interest in secret with great passion. I posed in front of the mirror, studied the facial expressions and angles I thought worked best for me. I snapped away with my borrowed camera and spent all the money that came my way on developing the pictures I had taken – of myself. It was a very narcissistic period: I thank my lucky stars those were the days before Instagram or Facebook!

I wanted to tell you this because the process of focusing on what is difficult yet meaningful

has often been the way for me to get somewhere in life. This has, of course, meant that there are significant gaps here and there in my learning, and my career may not have followed the path I might otherwise have intended. But tragic or not, something was borne out of that school course; an interest that actually provided me with an initial foundation on which to build; an education – albeit a fairly limited and convoluted one – but still something giving, worthwhile and substantial. Throughout the years I've found it important to remember that it is absolutely possible to work and gain knowledge without concepts, specific rules or extensive theoretical structures.

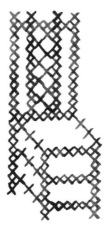

fine little day

Around the same time that I was finishing my studies at HDK School of Design and Crafts in Gothenburg in 2007, I discovered what a blog was. The idea that with just a few clicks of a button you could publish text and images online that someone else could see seemed to me, initially, like something incredible. I started my own blog called Fine Little Day. I liked the awkwardness in the sentence; it felt wrong but right, both at the same time.

The blog came to be a place far away from cynicism, where I could indulge in daydreams, communicate with interesting people all over the world, and put a silver lining on the everyday. I blogged about pictures I'd found at flea markets, images from an exhibition at the Röhsska Museum, an old stool I found intriguing. I began tentatively and inexpertly. After a while I began to touch on subjects like outsider art, folk art or art made by children. I visited people's homes and places of work, and photographed and compiled the images into blog series. Sometimes I posted about children's books or about other people's blogs and work.

It was all a spontaneous, diffuse and uncategorized mess, accompanied by notes in 'Swenglish'. Seven years later the blog still exists without a clear agenda and strong conceptual stance. This has suited me perfectly – I feel free and happy this way.

The same year as I started Fine Little Day, I made a poster for the illustration trade magazine *Tecknaren* and as payment for the commission I got a few hundred printed posters. What they had thought I would do with them is a mystery. However, it did encourage me to open my first web shop as a way to try and get rid of them! It was a humble Etsy shop containing a single poster design. The small, kind and encouraging following of readers that I had acquired through my blog helped to spread the word (or picture) about that poster.

Suddenly, in the blink of an eye, the stock was cleared – I was bemused. It turned out that a larger design blog had written about the poster, and then people started not just blogging about the poster, but also about Fine Little Day. And then the first job offer arrived.

The company wanted me to go to Italy to style images for a large, well-known nappy manufacturer. After that commissions began to appear from all kinds of unexpected parts of

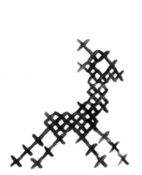

the world; clients came from Japan, the USA, Australia, Belgium and France, among other places. 'Wow!', I thought, and suddenly I could buy bread and butter and pay the rent, all thanks to continuous commissions stemming from the blog.

The years running the blog have been intense but rewarding. While I might forget all the details, I won't forget what the blog has meant to me personally. Apart from hundreds of thousands of camera exposures, a huge mess on my hard drives and a miserably flat bottom, blogging has made it possible for me to work with something that feels engaging and stimulating. It has meant that I have made friends and acquaintances in all corners of the globe; that I have largely been able to control my own time and that I have been able to spend a lot of time with my near and dear ones, which in my world translates to me having been able to fulfil some kind of basic vision of meaning in life. Hallelujah!

For me it's mostly about image and form – the surface, if you like – but also about lifestyle, about noticing and making use of things, and about objects that are sustainable and accessible. Superimposed, honest, thoughtless, wise, diffuse, eye-opening, unnecessary or important?

In this book I will occasionally draw on things from my years with Fine Little Day and also show new projects and things that talented friends have contributed. I will scatter images wildly through its pages. I have never been a fan of the advice, 'Kill your darlings', instead I prefer the sound of 'Keep it, however arbitrary', which feels more cheerful and permissive.

So expect digression that is untroubled and without deeper reasoning. The images, the din, the life that is presented within this book's covers, are about impression and expression, and have been captured or created in an attempt to embrace a kind of passion and creativity. The hope is, at least to some extent, to encourage and enthuse those who are leafing through its pages.

/Elisabeth Dunker

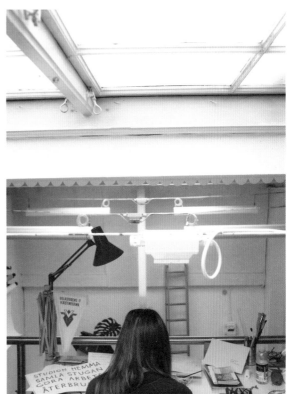

THE STUDIO

I wasn't meant to have a studio or workspace. I liked staying in my room, working with my children and everyday projects around me whenever I could, and when I felt like it. Then it became too cramped with stuff everywhere. I got the studio together with a colleague. We were enthusiastic. We were going to have a mezzanine and a skylight, spacious and bright. And then suddenly I got the feeling I had bitten off more than I could chew – the rent was so high! My humble thanks to all you good souls who, throughout the years, have shared your space with me and my miscellaneous, hoarded junk.

Klara
Bothén

Birgit & Benny's
Jenny Lundén
sits here

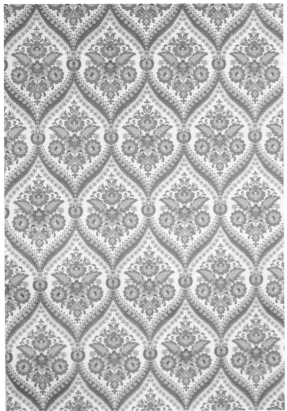

I sit here

Granliden mittens

In 1982, natural dyeing using plants was very popular. Courses and workshops on the subject were held across the country, and my mother, Christina, and grandmother, Ulla-Britta, were quick to jump on the bandwagon. That summer they dyed wool under clear skies by the summer cabin at Granliden. The water for the dye was collected from the lake at the bottom of the hill, and the plants were picked from the local area: heather, wild rosemary, birch leaves, cow parsley and reed flower, to name but a few. Thirty years later, despite diligent knitting, we still had a whole load of yarn left over, and I thought it was time to use it up. That is how the mittens came about.

As a designer I've made it my mission to make use of old, found materials and work them into something new. I want to make everything go one extra round and to find new values, surprising effects and preferably a good story. My mother and grandmother started and I continue their work. The saturated but delicate colours, combined with the simple design, provide a link between then and now, and together with the underlying story about the dyeing venture in the pine forests of Värmland, the mittens have become an example of how you, with relatively simple means, can give a new lease of life to old junk.

/Klara Bothén

Photography by Christina Bothén.

17

Mogu ♡

A Japanese artist, Mogu Takahashi, came to visit. She was putting on an exhibition in the studio. I had booked her a room at the Epidemic of Art in Gothenburg, and she borrowed a bike that she used to cruise around town. Mogu brought things that she had made in Japan, but mostly she embellished the things she found on location, using drawing, painting, collage, and sculpture. She painted on blocks, crockery, textiles, tiles, suitcases – yes, on all kinds of junk we had lying about. She decorated the junction box on the wall before she left, standing tiptoe on the stairs.

Illustration by Mogu Takahashi

My studiomate
Maja ⟶
Blomqvist's
tie-dyeing

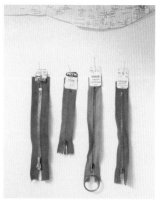

Further in:
Cecilia Pettersson
and Karin Strömberg

COLLECTING

I arrange treasures as they would appear in a shopping feature in a magazine. I don't always know a lot about them, often nothing at all. They are acquired, received as gifts, or borrowed because I've been enchanted by them, falling for them head-first. In an almost depraved manner I organize, study and arrange crockery according to its colour, along with piles of mismatched textiles, woolly socks and, of course, potholders – even though I can't crochet or knit – but perhaps that's precisely why. There is, after all, an abundance of hand-crocheted tablecloths, doilies and potholders at flea markets and in second-hand shops around Sweden. How did they end up there? When did they lose their value? I almost feel ashamed when I hand over as little as 20 kronor for four prime potholders. Usually they are astonishingly cheap and outrageously nice to look at.

The handcrafted wooden objects that I find sometimes feature signatures that have been mercilessly worn down by time. When I read 'Axel 1956', I imagine a youth who has carved and sandpapered, and perhaps given the item to his mother as a Christmas present? Ignorantly, I rarely ponder about the origins of these objects, it's what they express that interests me. It's about composition, sentimentality and positioning. I contemplate without needing to know more. I admit that at times it has been tricky to move freely around certain rooms, but keeping things isn't a necessity, and neither have I had to seek therapy because of my tendency to bring home a lot of stuff. Self-diagnosis: highly acquisitive, weak in character.

It says "handmade, handpainted
and SV, SO ceramics."

Ceramics by
Jennie Tuominen

Birch bark!

TONÅRING

I wonder where this comes from? Perhaps it was a souvenir from a holiday in Morocco, Egypt or Greece?

Beaded baskets

Things that don't leave me indifferent: plastic beads, especially in the form of a small basket, preferably with a handle. We used to call them 'Indian beads', and an Internet search will throw up the names 'Nabbi' or 'Hama' beads.

In any case, these remnants of the 1970s aren't just testimony to a crafting spirit gone by, but in all their homespun glory they still give happiness to pattern-hankering nostalgics today.

OPQRS
XYZ

Eftertryck förbjudes

Monica
MÄRK
BOK
MED MONOGRAM OCH
MÖNSTER I KORSSTYGN
2

GAMLESTADENS · FABRIKERS · AKTIEBOLAG · GÖTEBORG

702

ABC
DEF
KLMN
BCD
BC

KORSSTYGN

HS

UTGIVARE: HOLGER STJERNSTRÖM, MALMÖ

ok
MÖNSTER
M.M.

ABC
Bokstavens mittlinjer sys i stja
IJKL
Bladen kan också fyllas med
RST

ÖM
NSA MELÉN

ABCDEF
GHJKLM

AB   CD   EF   GK

IJ   KL   MN   OP

QR   ST   UV   WX

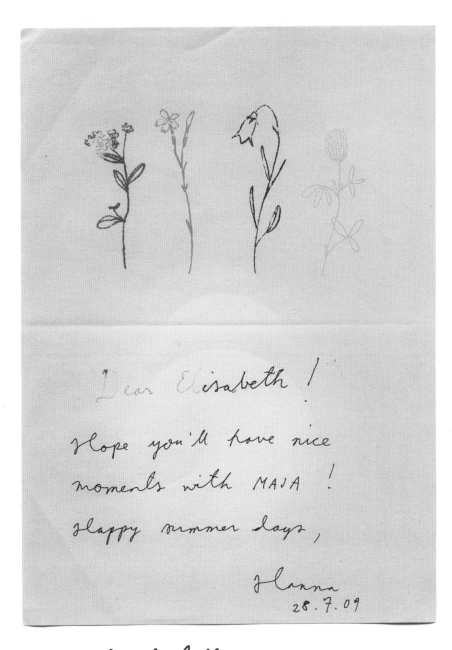

Dear Elisabeth !

Hope you'll have nice
moments with MAJA !

Happy summer days,

Hanna
28.7.09

The loveliest letter.
From Hanna Alajärvi

35

Blue crockery

Books

Because, among other things, it can contribute to cramped spaces and can foster unhealthy hoarding tendencies, I'm actually against bringing home too much stuff, but I just CAN'T walk past beautiful old books from the 1950s and 1960s like these and pretend that nothing has happened. And that's that.

Hand-bound treasure I came across during a visit to Mr and Mrs Håkan and Åsa Wettre.

AT HOME

The children were still little when we moved in. They didn't throw balls around, jump up and down on the floors or anything like that, even though our (ex-) neighbour claimed that that must be the case. In fact, we felt that we had to be unusually strict, and not allow too much banging in the dining room at meal times, or shrieks of joy when one had claimed victory over the other in a game of Ludo. This was the downside of being in an apartment block where there was someone with large, sensitive ears living underneath you. It put a proper dampener on our spirits to start off with I can tell you.

We've now lived in our flat for over ten years; neighbours have come and gone while our family has put down roots. The walls in the living room were beautifully red when we moved in, but after a couple of years we decided we needed more light, and painted them white. We have also put up wallpaper to provide accent walls here and there.

Apart from that, no renovating craze has ever really taken hold here. We've never been able to replace the fully working kitchen just because we didn't like the look of it; instead we have fixed and patched things together, and adapted ourselves to what was already here. It's lucky that we like things used and patinated, because here the floors squeak and the paint is peeling. In terms of interior design we are talking a mismatch of styles and eras.

Yes, you could use a load of stock phrases if you wanted to. I could try and gather all the expressions together here, or I could just show you what it looks like instead.

"Vårklockor"
(Spring bells)
Designed by
Josef Frank

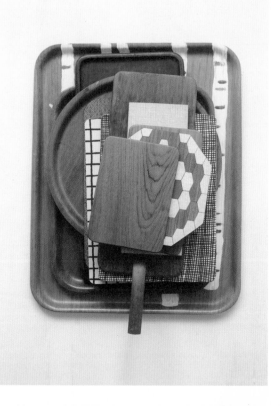

SALAD

Celery
Iceberg lettuce
Red lentils
Rapeseed oil
Lemon
Salt
black pepper

This is what it looks like in a bedroom where the idea of feng shui has never really caught on.

EXTRA PRETTY!

"Found this dress in a second hand shop some days ago. Instant love! The fabric is hand printed and the dress is tailor made, one copy, with nice details, as the removable upper part and the clothed buttons. Came home, tried it on, couldn't wear it! So, if you like it as much as I do, and if you are a small 38, let me know, and I will give it away for the cost of shipping."

My heart stopped when I saw it for the first time, and skipped a beat when I learned that the owner wanted to give it away. Thank you once again, Lena!

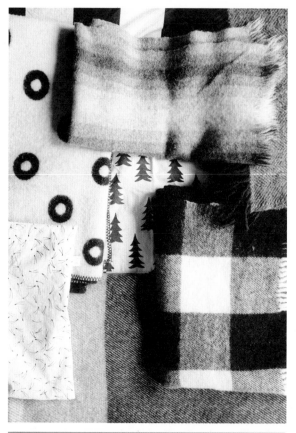

Plumping, pottering and photographing.
When you are showing other people how
you live, you can go around plumping up the
cushions, rearranging the furniture around
and nonchalantly scattering a few objects
around. Alternatively you can just stand up from
wherever you happen to be sitting, look around
and take it all in. I show pictures of how we live
all the time. It's a bubble. It's both navel-gazing
and some sort of illness. It works as a canvas to
paint on and also as therapy.

"121/395 View from Linnégatan 34 of Viktoriaskolan in Gothenburg." Mona Johansson, 1979.
I read about Mona Johansson on the Internet – born in Gothenburg 1924. Studied both in France and in Italy but showed more affection for Gothenburg and Varberg. She died in 2010. I've found a lot of pictures by Mona Johansson, all with street motifs and landscapes, but this is the only one I've bought.

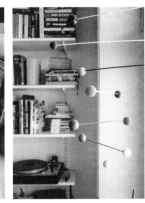

Grandma's old tablecloth, a ripped summer duvet, the fabric for that bag that was never sewn and other scraps.

picture wall

· ·

Arrange the pictures on the floor first. Use a
spirit level and taped guides if you need to.
Take a photo to help you remember, and
then get them up on the wall.

Designed by Kindra Murphy

Cloud by Alessandra Taccia

Self-adhesive, removable wallpaper and raindrop stickers – in case you change your mind, or just fancy something new. Not that long ago she was ten and had her portrait drawn on a doily by Gini Helie. Our beloved child. From a toddler to a teenager and young adult, in the same room.

A 12-year-old lives here

• •

Ask me about what's on the surface. Why do I have this obsession with what things look like? Why this disproportionate focus on beauty and aesthetics? What is it all about? Well, at any point in history has there been a community in the world that didn't care about adorning, polishing or arranging? Haven't human beings always decorated their homes, tools and clothing, or plaited their hair for no other reason than to be looked at?

But is it all just about status, authority and cultural capital? Those things can seem banal and unnecessary, depending on how far you zoom out, and from which perspective you consider them. Is it about allowing ourselves to be distracted, to forget about the mundane aspects of life? Is it about caring and appreciation? Or is it simply just a part of being human? I don't know. But I do know that when I see something pleasant, attractive or beautiful, I am engaged. And that thinking about beautiful things can help me feel calm and comforted, and make everything seem a little easier.

RE-USING

Because it eases anxiety.
Because it's a good thing to do.

And it's satisfying –
creating something new
from something old.

Sri Lankan doormats

I'd like to show you these fantastic doormats that I found in Sri Lanka a few years ago. The rugs are sewn primarily by poor women in rural areas and are made from discarded textiles and remnants from textile factories. The textiles are cut into strips and sewn together to make squares or circles, and then added onto a heavier backing fabric (often denim).

Quite often you can see that the fabric scraps really have been well used – in places they are stained and patched together.

Something else which is nice about these treasures (as well as being perfect for use as chair pads by the way), is that they often look even lovelier on the back than they do on the front.

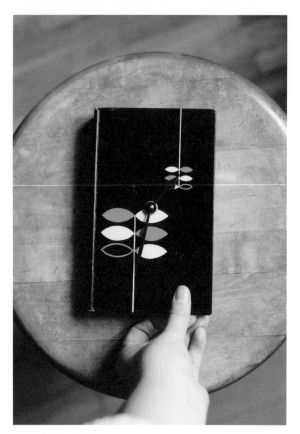

book clocks

· ·

This is nifty! By cutting out a hole in the book pages for the mechanism, and attaching the hands on the cover, Hilda Grahnat (photographer, designer and multi-talent) makes clocks out of books like these. Visit www.hildagrahnat.com for more information.

Photography by Hilda Grahnat.

In theory you can cut out block patterns from anything: just cover it in paint and use it to print onto paper or textiles. My block prints have simple shapes that I cut out from rubber-like soft sheets, also known as craft foam. But you could also use potatoes (make sure they are big ones).

BLOCK-PRINTING

1. Cut the shape you want out of craft foam, using a knife or scissors. Or cut the shape out from the base of a cork or the cut side of a potato.
2. If you're working with craft foam, put double-sided tape on the back of it and attach it to a block of some kind that you can grip easily.
3. Place a piece of cardboard underneath the fabric to avoid the paint bleeding through to the surface below.

4. Dab your printing block with fabric paint using a sponge scourer, and then press it down onto the fabric.
5. Leave the paint to dry before making it permanent with an iron (use the temperature guidelines on the paint's packaging).

You will need:

- Scissors or a knife
- Craft foam, potatoes, cork or something similar
- Fabric paint
- Sponge scourers
- Fabric to print on

Tip: You can find craft foam on Ebay.

patch-work quilt

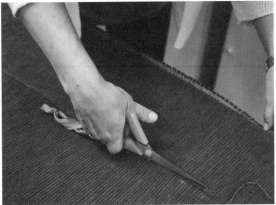

Not that long ago this was nothing but a couple of bags full of mismatched textiles and personal memories that had been left in a wardrobe for an unreasonably long period of time. Now - thanks to a gifted sewing friend - it has transformed into a lovely patchwork blanket. Even though we're not forced to make use of scraps today as we had to do in the old days, patchwork quilts are still appreciated, and sewn. Thank goodness. Here is an alternative way to make your own patchwork quilt.

1. Choose your fabrics and decide on the measurements for your quilt.
2. Decide on the size of patches you want and work out how many you will need. Zigzag the edges.
3. Arrange the patches in the order you want them.
4. Pin and sew the patches together one row at a time. Press the seams flat using an iron.
5. Sew the rows together to create the front of your quilt.
6. Cut out a backing material and a lining material.
7. Zigzag the edges of the backing material if needed.
8. Place the front and the back together, right sides facing and with the lining on top. Sew around the quilt but leave an opening so you can turn the quilt right side out.
9. Turn the quilt the right way round and sew up the opening.

tips

- If your quilt is made from scraps it's a good idea to use a stencil (made from cardboard, for example) when cutting out the patches.
- If it's going to be a big one, divide the quilt into smaller sections to make it easier to handle.
- A cutting mat, ruler and rotary cutter (instead of scissors) will help if you are using a lot of the same fabric.
- Leave enough seam allowance to 'secure' the seams.
- Make sure the lining and the fabrics are washed so that they don't shrink afterwards.
- Keep the lining in place by quilting (sewing around or through it using straight stitch) through all the layers.

Potholder blankets

· ·

Hey! Look at these – children's blankets made
from potholders. The best present ever!
Handmade, wonky treasures. Personal, to
say the least.

Sewing a potholder blanket

For the absolute best result, sew the potholders together by hand: this will make the overlapping neater. First, sew them into rows, and then attach together by hand. It's a good idea to start with the squares; the round potholders are trickier to attach. If you want a backing material, place the finished blanket on top of a piece of fabric and cut out the desired shape (remembering to place the fabric so that you get the side you want facing out). Attach the backing material by sewing a welt all around the blanket. If you want to make something larger, such as a throw for a double bed, it will take a little longer but just think how stylish it will look!

Tips and needlework: Anna Melkersson, designer at Knätofs.

decorating books

· ·

If you find it difficult to put pen to a blank,
white sheet of paper, what about a surface
with structure and patina? Something that will
also add colour to your bookshelf. If you're
serious about it, read the book too. Pencil,
pastels, watercolour, nail varnish – use
whatever you've got!

wooden spoons

What do you think about these instead of Barbie dolls? No visible waistlines and fewer flexible limbs, far more character and no less realistic. Besides, they're fun to make. Use acrylics, crayons, pencil or felt-tip pens – freehand. Anything goes.

painting textiles

· ·

Acrylic paint is amazing stuff: durable, quick to dry and water soluble, it works both for opaque and more transparent finishes (if mixed with water). It also adheres to all kinds of surfaces, even a shabby old nightgown and a pair of tattered dungarees.

THE CABIN

I'm going to tell you about our summer cabin. I've lived in an apartment my whole life, but I've always longed for a small house with a patch of land. Of course, this is all about an idealistic view of a rural life, where you dig the soil with the children, rake leaves and collect fallen fruit from the yard, and then, after a rich stew with lots of garlic, you sit in front of a crackling fire with a thick book in your lap.

It was a dream I was determined to fulfil, but one year I realized that if something didn't happen soon, I was going to turn 40 and still be no closer to having my summer cabin. Some time before my birthday I booked a trip for the family: we were going to Småland where there was a house for sale.

The chances of us getting it weren't that great, however: we had no prior connections to the village or to the county of Småland; not everyone was convinced; and we didn't have any saved funds. But the place was perfect – it gave us good vibes in every single way. And besides, our mortgage application was approved by the bank. We could hardly believe it, but a few weeks later, in August, we moved in!

There was an orchard, period tile stoves, flowery wallpaper, wooden floors and an Aga stove in the kitchen. An absolute idyll! It was clear that this place was sewn with my dreams used as a thread. The wallpaper has been there for decades, and we also got to keep the furniture, tools, crockery and even the clothes in the chest of drawers.

Småland

Painting a picture, that's what I'm thinking. We're not exactly standing in the middle of some kind of Astrid Lindgren idyll. But we are all allowed to pretend a little, aren't we? Because it will become bittersweet and nostalgic regardless.

The chicken shed

The apartment-dweller in me wanted to learn how to identify different plants and how to cultivate the land, but the soil here is not good for growing, especially not for amateurs like us. We discovered the area has the same climate as Gästrikland in the north. The dry-stone walls in Småland are strong and wide. Our garden is allowed to grow wild: the grass is always a little too high and the flowerbeds aren't tended to. I'm not trying to make excuses, it's what we can manage.

cobbled doilies

Handsewn using needle and thread. You don't have to be very thorough. Pin the doilies together first. The good thing is that they will hold together with just a few stitches. And they will appear almost magical, hanging up in a window, with the sun shining through.

More patch-work

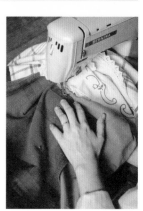

This is a cheat's version of a patchwork quilt, very useful if you don't have enough time or patience, or just aren't feeling that dexterous. Take an old bed sheet, pin on some patches and just zigzag to sew them together. You'll get a thinner throw, perhaps it will sag a little and be a bit bulky in places, but it will look nice nonetheless.

• •

Summer

I wasn't happy with what I wrote for this page at first; I rewrote it several times but then I deleted it completely. I wanted to write something about drinking red wine from plastic cups, about a deserted beach and a small fox that we'd sometimes spot at the edge of the forest.

But I got it all mixed up because this particular afternoon, my friend K and I had braved the cold and drizzle to go down to the Storesjön jetty, because K wanted to have a swim. This gave me the chance to photograph someone who would otherwise be very camera shy – there was absolutely no way I was getting into water that was below 25 degrees. Determined and – as it seemed to me – totally fearless, she removed her clothes, ran across the boards so that her hair was blowing behind her and, at the end of the jetty, she jumped.

Boldly, without a flinch, she just plunged right into the water.

Then she was cold, I could tell from the hairs that were standing straight up on her arms when she climbed back up the ladder. I sat down next to her on the jetty, shivering and waiting while she lit a cigarette (something I have never even tried) – if you can believe that!

Now while I am disclosing, as it appears in writing at least, just how strait-laced I am (I don't drink coffee either), I should also admit I'm a bundle of nerves in the evenings, and as a rule I never go out after nine o'clock at night. You can't see anything when it's dark outside, and it's also when unknown creatures go creeping around. That's just the way I am.

Nyaby Västergård. Built in 1933, originally the house accommodated two families. The old stove on the top floor still stands proudly in a corner, the outhouse is still there too, and the forest.

Autumn

Here we are keeping ourselves busy by tracing our footprints onto an old cushion cover, using fabric crayons that we bought cheaply from a charity shop. The children are sulking and are longing to go home to games consoles, computers and a heated apartment. The walls here aren't insulated to modern standards.

Once the snow came: like a glistening, crystalline blanket, it was there when we woke up. Pushed down behind a kitchen counter top we found some treasures: a Flemish tapestry and a knitting pattern for Kattens Lovikka mittens. Did anyone knit them and make a snowball with them?

BESKRIVNING
6592

LOVIKKA-vantar

**Kattens
LOVIKKA
(med stödtråd)**

Garnåtgång:

Storlek	8 år	(12 år)	dam	(herr)
	1	(1½)	2	(2) hg.

Strumpstickor: AERO nr 4 eller 4½ beroende på handlaget

6592

MAKING

Wallpaper
by Cecilia
Pettersson

Mobile

• •

Et voilà: a tree mobile, or something like that.
The fun thing about making mobiles is that you
can hang up any old thing and it will still look
nice. The rusty iron hoop we picked up from a
pile of discarded junk we found on a walk one
day. The leaves are pressed, and the rest are
miscellaneous bits and bobs that you can find
pretty much anywhere. I attached the elements
using clear fishing wire; I made little holes in the
leaves, ran the fishing wire through and then
tied a knot. The hoop is attached to kitchen
string so that it can hang from the ceiling.

Crochet potholder

How many potholders do you need? It depends. To handle hot pots and pans and other things in the kitchen, let's say two, four at the most. But if you have a patchwork blanket in mind, or something equally as grandiose, perhaps you might need more in the region of 278. So really you can have as many potholders as you like, and you can get started straight away. Here's one way to do it.

1. Start by creating chain stitches using a white yarn. Make a slip knot and place the knot on the hook. Make a stitch by catching the yarn around the hook and draw the yarn through the loop. Repeat in the same way until you've got 30 chain stitches in total. Then make one extra chain stitch to allow for turning to the next row.

2. Next, create double crochet stitches: insert your hook into both loops on the second stitch, catch the yarn around the hook – you've now got two loops on the hook – and pull the yarn through both loops. Continue to make double crochet stitches to the end of the row and turn using an extra chain stitch.

3. Crochet six rows with white yarn, then switch to red: cut off the white yarn (save approximately 10cm) and begin to crochet with red yarn, starting from the turning stitch. Crochet six rows with each colour until you've got three white and three red stripes, making a total of 30 rows. Secure by pulling the yarn through the last stitch and then cut off the end. Secure all loose ends by sewing them into the stitches.

4. If you want, double crochet around the edge of the potholder, and make a loop made from chain stitches.

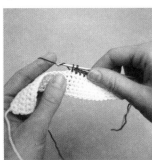

Text and instructions by Klara Bothén.

How to make a beaded jar

You will need:

- A jar
- Beads
- Clear, elastic thread
- Blunt needle
- Glue
- Scissors
- Pegboard (if you're making a lid)

1. Start by choosing which jar you'd like to use as your base.
2. Estimate how many beads you will need to cover the height of the jar. The easiest way is to thread them up to see how many you will need to get the right height. If you're also making a lid it's a good idea to leave approximately 1cm at the top of the lid clear of beads. You'll need an even number of beads to make it work.
3. Once you've threaded an even amount of beads to fit your jar, it's time to start shaping the jar. When you start on row two you will weave in every second bead from the second row. If you count from the first bead in the next row you will add bead number 1, 3, 5, 7 ... and so on (the first bead in the second row will sit next to the last bead in the first row) at the same time as you thread the needle through the beads on the previous row, instead of bead 2, 4, 6, 8 ... and so on. Continue for the following rows.

4. Continue in the same way and arrange the beads into a pattern of your choice. If you run out of thread you can just tie another piece on using a double knot. It's easiest to handle an arm-length thread. Pull the thread quite tight as you go along, to make the jar hold together nicely. When you change thread, it's a good idea to strengthen the knot with a dollop of glue, as the elastic thread tends to come undone more easily than sewing thread (the knot will be hidden inside the beads anyway).
5. When the weave of beads is large enough to reach around the jar, preferably with quite a tight fit, you need to stitch it together with the beads from the first row. Tie a knot and secure with glue. Make the lid by placing beads onto the pegboard. Measure the size by ensuring that the beads on the pegboard are one bead larger than the jar you're using as a base. Iron together the beads on the pegboard.
6. Extend the outer row by threading on a few rows of beads using the same technique as you used for the jar. Thread through the beads on the outer row of the lid. Make sure the ironed side is facing downwards to form the inside of the lid.

Photography and instructions by Lena Skogsberg.

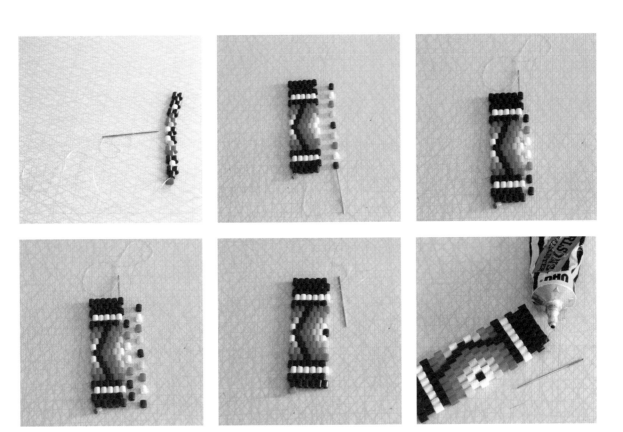

Pressing plants

One summer I spent all my time bending down until my back was crooked and my neck was stiff, always at the ready with a plastic bag in my hand. I had found an antique in the attic of the cabin: an old botanical press.

Sometime later, when I came across a collection of dried plants from 1937–41, which comprised an incredible number of well-preserved specimens and beautiful handwritten notes about where, when and what they were, I became even more enthusiastic – all kinds of plants were thrown into the press once again. I wasn't concerned about including the roots or making mental notes; I had picked them in Småland, that was enough. However seriously you want to approach your botanical collection, it's a very rewarding way to preserve the summer.

You will need:

- Plants
- Protective paper (newspaper or normal drawing paper works fine)
- Blotting paper or other absorbent paper
- A botanical press or some heavy books
- Glue for attaching the plants (optional)

FLORA SUECICA

1. It's best to pick the plants on a dry day so that they are not too wet to start off with. Include the root if you want to. Press them on the same day they are picked or they will wilt.

2. Use a folded, protective paper sheet and spread the plants out over it. Try to place flowers and leaves so that they will be pressed into a nice shape and aren't overlapping. Clean them if necessary. Place blotting paper in between the layers to soak up any liquid.

3. Arrange layers of blotting paper and the protective paper containing the plants in the botanical press. The plants should always sit between two layers of the protective paper so that they aren't damaged. To start off with you'll need to replace the blotting paper every day in order to preserve as much of the plants' colour as possible and to prevent mould from developing. The more often you change the blotting paper, the quicker the plants will dry. The amount of time the plants should stay in the press depends on their thickness.

Tip: When the plant no longer feels cold against the skin, it's dry.

cutting paper

I know this is nursery craft – folding and cutting paper, making garlands and snowflakes. Old newspapers ... I didn't use them here but that would be very nice, don't you think? Or other types of patterned or coloured recycled paper.

PEEKING IN

· ·

Here are some places I've visited and people I've met. A glimpse into the world of warm, wise and exciting people; creatives, all the way to their fingertips. First, a visit to a family who live in an old shop; then a peek into the home of authors and artists Håkan and Åsa Wettre; next, a small allotment house, my colleague Anna Backlund's amazing place; and finally the magnificent Marianne Hallberg. A few posts from Fine Little Day that could be bookmarked as personal favourites - coming right up.

This is an apartment with a shop section that once housed a bookshop. Today a small family of three lives here. Two floors; French doors with glass blocks, amongst other things. Who would have guessed that such a gorgeous flat could be found right in the middle of the Majorna district of Gothenburg? Not me.

Håkan &
Åsa Wettre

Some homes you find difficult to leave because you feel as if you've ended up in the right place, and because the people who live there put no limits on creativity. One of these places belongs to Håkan and Åsa Wettre. It is almost disrespectful to squeeze this wonderful place into just a couple of pages.

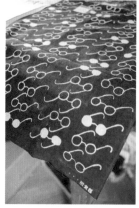

Anna
Dacklund
residence

Here is an attic, a loft, built from scrap wood, mostly fir and plywood. A space that was almost forgotten but in the end was transformed into the heart of the house. It smells nice here. Anna Backlund is a designer, the rug on the floor is one of her creations.

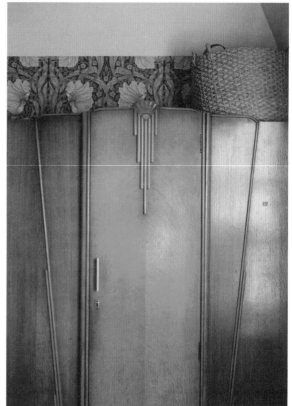
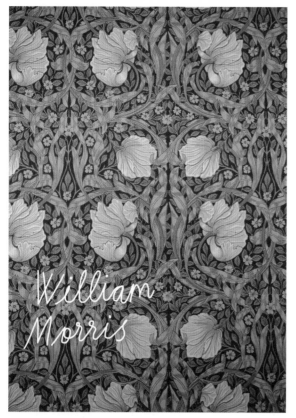

William
Morris

Camilla
Engman
↓

Jordgubbsgången (The strawberry walk)

It's hard to think of anything nicer than looking after your own plot of land in the city. Growing things is the focus here of course, but it's the little house that you would fall in love with. Two adults and two children who fell for the colour, the windows and the wood-fired stove, come here every weekend; the summer holidays are filled with bare-foot play and simple living. On an afternoon in April, there are freshly picked anemones and newly baked scones.

Marianne
Hallberg

VARDAGSARTEFAKT
BEGREPPET HÄNGER
NÄRA SAMMAN MED
MATERIELL KULTUR
ORDET GRUNDADES
1821

ARTEFAKT
ARS = KONST
FACER = GÖRA, TILLVERKA
BETYDER EGENTLIGEN
KONSTGJORT FÖREMÅL
TILLVERKAT AV
MÄNNISKAN
PRYL

Marianne Hallberg does what she wants – you realize that as soon as you meet her. Neither does she make pottery in the way that you'd expect. Her rolled stoneware with a white tin-based glaze, decorated with cobalt oxide has a look that contrasts strikingly with other ceramics. I'm very fond of them. Her work can be found at the Rhösska Museum in Gothenburg, Sweden, the FuLe International Ceramic Art Museums (FLICAM) in China and at my place of course.

Like someone with itchy feet I'm always rushing around; it's okay to be free, it's okay to lose yourself as much as you want. Look at me, I'm playing! I refuse to feel ashamed and it makes me happy. When people call me on the phone and ask me to buy things I say, 'No thanks, I've got everything I need, I'm content, complete,' and it's almost always true. Perhaps I'm romanticizing things a little: am I a true individualist? Maybe. I certainly want to show solidarity and generosity, I also want to indulge in the things I find most interesting and make use of what is around me, go crazy, try things – without limits. In the early hours I squeeze myself into bed in between china bowls, rustling paper, open books and other forgotten stuff. And cat litter – always too late. I can't believe I make a living out of this! But it's also about appreciating life to a certain extent: because the world is ordinary, you want to have fun.

PLAYING, and more

playing

Essentials

I don't know how you spend your time off,
but here we're talking quality time deluxe.
Can you think of anything more rewarding
than spending an hour or two moving
flowers, leaves and petals around on
a piece of cardboard?
No, didn't think so.

Tip/inspiration:

Google "plant mandala"
or search the hashtag
#mandala on Instagram.

Henning Trollbäck

'Here on Söderöra, in the north Stockholm archipelago, we've had our houses since the 1970s. While renovating the kitchen in the smaller house, my mum took out a section of the old plasterboard above the door, with the wallpaper still attached. I liked the clove wallpaper, so I thought if I fixed the wall first perhaps I would paint something to go in its place. After repairing the wall I started mixing pigments, glue and chalk into authentic, old-fashioned distemper. It had a fantastic, beautiful matt finish that resembles gouache in its colour saturation.

I mixed together a green paint that matched the surrounding clove wallpaper fairly well and painted a base coat. After that I mixed one lighter and one darker green, as on the clove wallpaper, together with a few other colours. It felt good to sit and experiment with authentic pigment powder.

Then I went out into the garden and picked a few plants that are usually found growing with cloves, such as daisies and various weeds and small plants. And then I gathered a few others that I like, such as orpine, dandelion, lavender and stinging nettle and started to paint.'

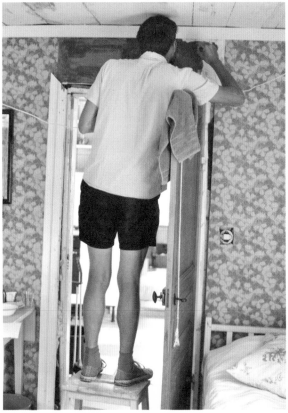

And then I gathered a
orpine, dandelion, love
and started to paint.

Henning Trollbäck

others that I like, such as

and stinging nettle

Doll's house

I'm building a shanty town, because one should never give up playing with doll's houses. Every cupboard, box and bag is a potential living space, like a mini-universe where things are manageable. If you have an old suitcase, saw out holes for doors and windows – I use one of those multi-tools. If you are thinking about buying one, get one with a lead and you won't have to wait for the battery to charge.

Please allow me to jump between subjects and land here and there, and present my ideas in the same fragmentary and arbitrary way that things actually occur, without attaching any deeper meaning to it. It's appropriate I think, to show examples of work that have emerged in the wake of a blogging era that today (or perhaps yesterday) has reached its peak.

I've never really been able to give a clear account of how I work. I don't have a set methodology, but instead I start in a different place every time. Neither do I have any particularly clever phrases to throw around when it comes to talking about the things that I've made. To put it simply, I work exploratively, according to trial and error.

And I'm constantly terrified that I will be caught – and exposed as a sham – at any time. You're calling yourself a designer, an artist? Ha! What a joke!

House of Rym

I'd like to tell you about the email that began: 'Dear Madam, I like your designs. Have you ever been to Tunisia? If not I think we need to arrange a visit for you to come here. What do you think my dear? If possible of course.' The message was binned – I get lots of strange emails. A few days later my colleague Anna Backlund called. She had received an email from Tunisia, she told me happily. 'They want me to come – you'd join me, wouldn't you?'

After some persuasion I was sitting on the plane. Even though I had my reservations until the very last minute. But I needn't have worried: at the airport we were greeted with big smiles by two young entrepreneurs (Zied and Rym), who took us out on various trips over the next few days. Unlike earlier commissions from clients located much closer to home, Anna and I gained a thorough insight into the production chain, and were also given the chance to have a say in the choice of materials and production methods. The commission would be a big job; the idea was that we should establish a brand, and everything that goes along it. The plan was to combine ancient Tunisian handicrafts with Swedish design. In principle Anna and I would have free rein to create the concept and content, and the idea was that the whole thing should happen quickly.

When the plane landed back in Sweden a few days later, we had made a list of talented colleagues we would call, we had come up with ideas for a collection and a recycled line, and we had also agreed that the project would be called 'House of Rym'.

Homemade cement tiles. Designs by Emma von Brömssen, Cecilia Pettersson, Anna Backlund and Elisabeth Dunker.

We went on a trip to **ORUST**, to get some inspiration

An island in western Sweden

— Hannah Schön and her little one, Fia Miari, Anna Backlund and me.

Cook up a simple fish soup (serves 4)

2 garlic cloves, crushed
½ leek, sliced
1 brown onion, chopped
2 carrots, coarsely sliced
3 potatoes, diced
100ml white wine
2 stock cubes
200ml crème fraîche
Herbs of your choice
400g white fish

1. Sweat the garlic, leek, onion, carrots and potatoes for a few minutes.
2. Add 600ml water, the wine and then add the stock cubes. Leave to boil for about 5 minutes.
3. Stir in the crème fraîche and any herbs you want to use, such as thyme. Add the fish.
4. Simmer gently for another 5 minutes, and enjoy!

Kauniste

· ·

Can you imagine a lake like a mirror, nestled between the trees, with someone fishing from a small jetty? And right in the middle of the gleaming lake: a water ballet. Finnish company Kauniste (look them up) asked me to make this blanket for them.

Photography by Hilda Grahnat.

Thank you, Leif Södergren!

Hand printed
by Lena Corwin

BIG THANKS

(let's go with alphabetical order)

Anna Backlund
Anna Melkersson
Cattis Skoglund
Hilda Grahnat
Håkan och Åsa Wettre
Johanna Sjöstrand
Katarina Karlsson
Klara Bothén
Lena Skogsberg
Malin Liveståhl
Marianne Hallberg
Mogu Takahashi
Ulrika E. Engberg

Ceramics by
Claire Loder

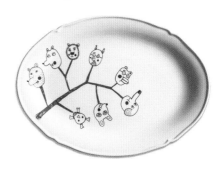

Dennis, Tovalisa & Otto Dunker ♡

First published in the United Kingdom in 2015 by
Pavilion
1 Gower Street
London
WC1E 6HD

Copyright © 2014 Elisabeth Dunker
Natur & Kultur, Stockholm

Distributed in the United States and Canada by
Sterling Publishing Co., Inc. 1166 Avenue of the Americas,
New York, NY 10036

All rights reserved. No part of this publication may be reproduced, stored in a
retrieval system or transmitted in any form or by any means, electronic, mechanical,
photocopying, recording or otherwise, without the prior written permission of the
copyright owner.

ISBN 978-1-910496-31-2

A CIP catalogue record for this book is available from the British Library.

10 9 8 7 6 5 4 3 2

Reproduction by Mission Productions Ltd, Hong Kong
Printed by 1010 Printing International Ltd, China

This book can be ordered direct from the publisher at www.pavilionbooks.com

● ●

Photography: Elisabeth Dunker, except pages 4, 66-67, 170-171 by Hilda Grahnat;
pages 154-155 by Annafia Hansson; and pages 16-17 by Christina Bothén.

The publisher would like to thank Frida Green for her work on this book.

First published in Sweden in 2014 by Natur & Kultur, Stockholm

www.nok.se
info@nok.se